21033259

This book to be returned on
the last date stamped b

REQUEST
19 SEP 1990

3 OCT 1990

24 DEC 1991

BOOK No. 21033259 CLASS No. 794

	1.	5.
CLACKMANNAN DISTRICT LIBRARY H.Q.	2.	6.
17 MAR STREET ALLOA FK10 1HT	3.	7.
	4.	8.

Design a Board Game

This booklet will help you to design your own board game.
There are four stages involved.

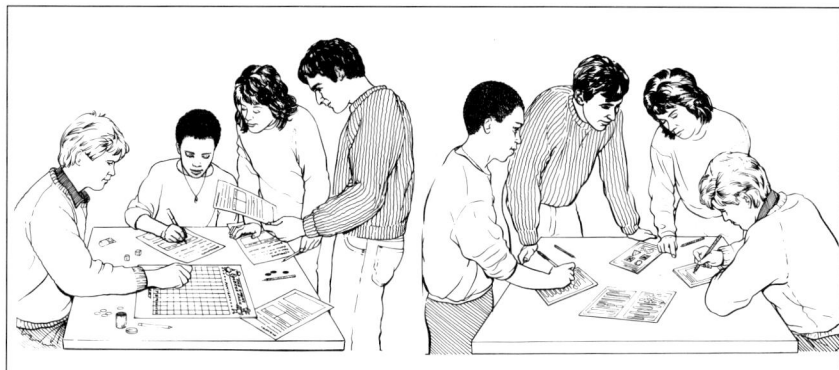

Stage 1
Looking at examples
pages 2–14

Stage 2
Developing your own ideas
pages 15–23

Stage 3
Making your game
pages 24–28

Stage 4
Testing and evaluating
pages 29–31

1

Stage 1 Looking at examples

To begin with, you will play some games that were invented by other people, to see what you can learn from them.

Later on, you will invent your own game.

Will you be able to make better games than these?

The games are called:		page
■ The Great Horse Race	1 to 12 players	4
■ Bugs	2 players	6
■ Goal	2 players	8
■ Treasure Island	2, 3 or 4 players	10
■ Honeycomb	2 players	12

You will also be asked to think about other games you have played.

STAGE 1

As you play each game, you have to fill in a copy of the 'Comments' sheet.

STAGE 1 AND STAGE 4

Comments

Name of the game _____

Filled in by _____

While you are playing, write down some good and bad features of it.

Good points	Bad points
It's a game of skill because... It's exciting because...	It's not fair because... It's boring because... The rules aren't clear because...

Play the game a few times.
Make a note of the result on the back of this sheet.
About how long did each game take? ☐ minutes
After you have played, say how you could improve the game.

make the counters smaller, and make them this shape...
Change the rule for winning to...
make the board look like this...

DESIGN A BOARD GAME
© Shell Centre for Mathematical Education/Joint Matriculation Board 1987

M1

STAGE 1

THE GREAT HORSE RACE

A game for 1 to 12 players.

What you need

The board, two dice and twelve counters to represent the horses

STAGE 1

Aim of the game

Twelve horses enter a race. The first one to pass the finishing line wins.

Rules

How to start

- Put the horses on their starting squares, labelled 1 to 12.

- Each player chooses a different horse.
  (If there are only a few players, then each player can choose two or three horses.) The remaining horses are still in the race – but no-one owns them.

How to play

- Throw the two dice, and add the scores
  (eg ⚀ ⚄ gives the number 8).

- The horse with that number moves *one* square forward.

- Keep throwing the dice.
  The horse which is first past FINISH is the winner.

- Play this game a few times.
- Each time you play, write down, on the back of your 'Comments' sheet, which horse comes 1st, 2nd, 3rd, and so on.

STAGE 1

BUGS

A game for 2 players.

What you need

A board, a dice and two counters to act as bugs.

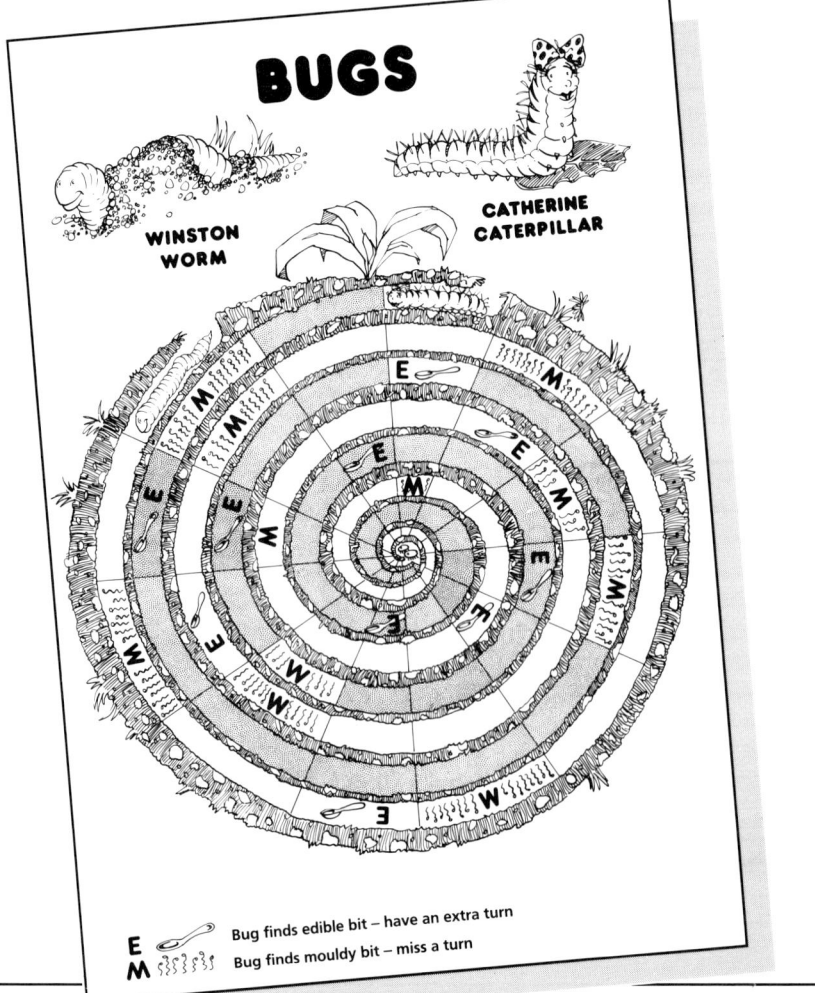

STAGE 1

What it's about

The apple has two tunnels leading to the core in the middle.

Each bug follows one tunnel.

Aim of the game

To reach the core first.

Rules

How to start

- Put the bugs on the two bug pictures.

How to play

- Take it in turns to throw the dice.
- Move your bug along your tunnel the number of spaces shown by the dice.
- If you land on an **M** (mouldy) space – miss a go.
- If you land on an **E** (edible) space – have an extra go.

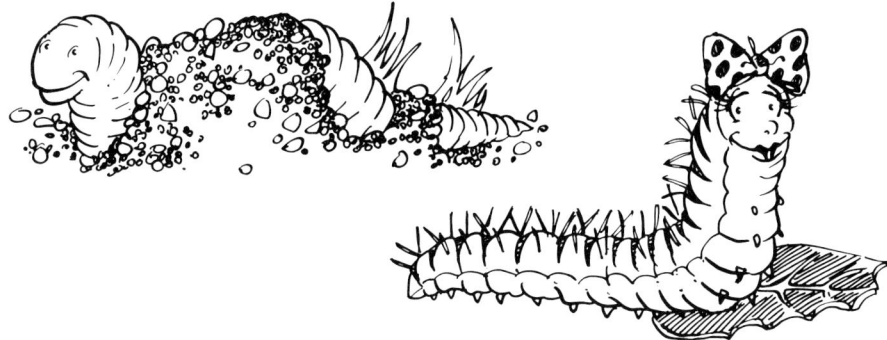

- Play this game a few times.
- Each time you play, write down, on the back of your 'Comments' sheet, whether Winston or Catherine wins.

STAGE 1

GOAL

A game for 2 players.

What you need

The board, a counter for the ball, a pack of playing cards.

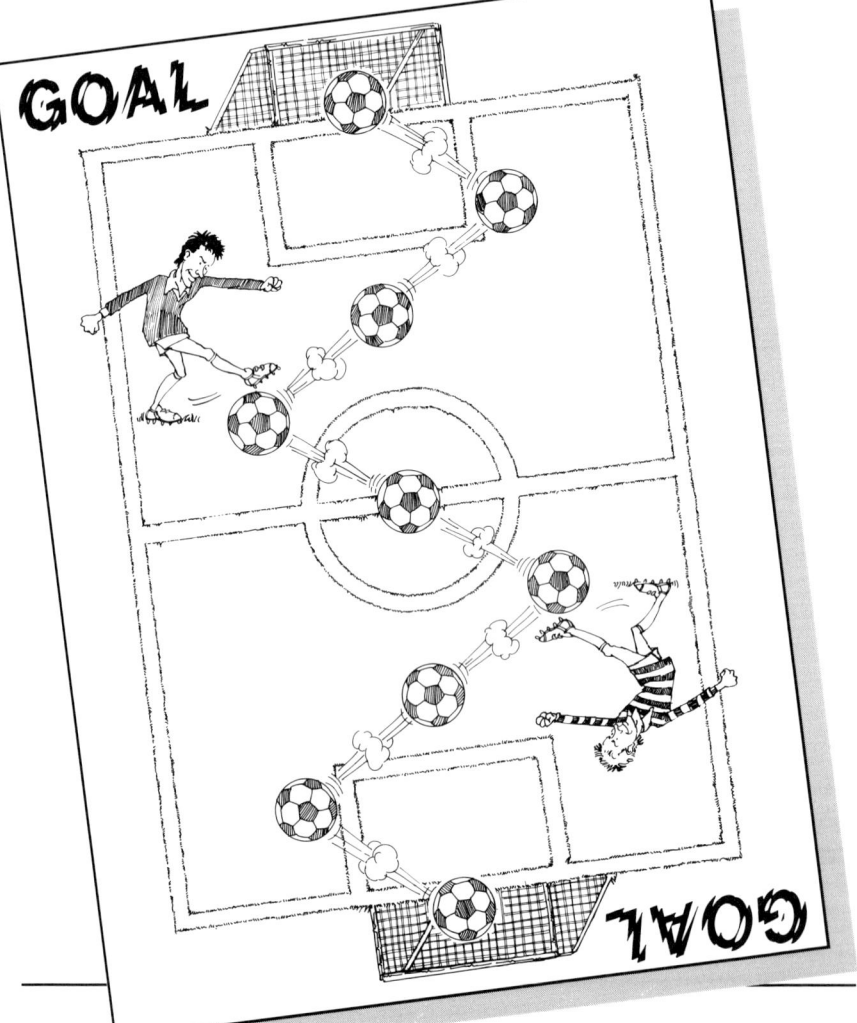

STAGE 1

What it's about	Aim of the game
This game is rather like hockey or football.	To score more goals than your opponent before time runs out.

Rules

How to start

- Place the ball in the centre circle.

- Give one player a *red* Ace, 2, 3, 4, 5, 6, 7, 8, 9 and 10.
  Give the other player a *black* Ace, 2, 3, 4, 5, 6, 7, 8, 9 and 10.
  (The rest of the cards are not used.)

How to move the ball

- Look at your cards.

- Now each choose a card and put it face down on the table.

- Both of you turn your cards over at the same time.

- If you have the higher value, move the ball one step towards your opponent's goal.

- Now each choose another card and put it face down on the table. Compare them as before.

Scoring goals

- You score when the ball reaches your opponent's goal. Then you replace the ball in the centre circle.

- Time runs out when both players have used up their ten cards. The person who has scored the most goals is the winner.

- Play the game a few times.
- Each time you play, write down, on the back of your 'Comments' sheet, whether the red or black team wins.

STAGE 1

TREASURE ISLAND

A game for 2, 3 or 4 players.

What you need

The board, a dice, four boats, twelve treasure rings, pack of 'Fight' cards.

STAGE 1

What it's about

The board shows the sea with four ports and a Treasure Island.

You have to sail to the Island Harbour and collect treasure.

You can attack other ships as well.

Aim of the game

To collect three treasure rings from Treasure Island and land them at your port.

Rules

How to start

- Start with your boats in your ports and the treasure on the island.
- Shuffle the 'Fight' pack and put the cards face down.
- Each player takes a card, but keeps the number on the card secret.

How to make a move

- Throw the dice in turns.

  You can move your boat any number of triangles up to the number on the dice.

- You collect treasure when you arrive at the HARBOUR on the island, but your boat can only carry one treasure ring at a time.

- If you land on a triangle next to a boat carrying treasure, you fight. You both show your 'Fight' card. The player with the highest score takes the treasure, the loser gets a free move of two triangles. Then put your cards to the bottom of the pack and take new ones.

- Play the game a few times.
- Each time you play, write down, on the back of your 'Comments' sheet, the name of the winning Pirate.

STAGE 1

HONEYCOMB

A game for 2 players.

What you need

The board, and a set of counters in two colours, one for the 'Worker' bees and one for the 'Drones'. 13 of each colour will be needed.

STAGE 1

What it's about

Two kinds of bee are trying to control a hive – the 'Workers' and the 'Drones'.

Aim of the game

The 'Drones' must try to make a connected path from the top to the bottom of the board. The 'Workers' must try to make a path from side to side.

Rules

- Take turns to put a counter on *any* empty hexagon. (You need not put your first counter at the edge; you need not put your counter next to the one before.)
- The examples show two winning paths.

Drones win in this example
Example A

Workers win in this example
Example B

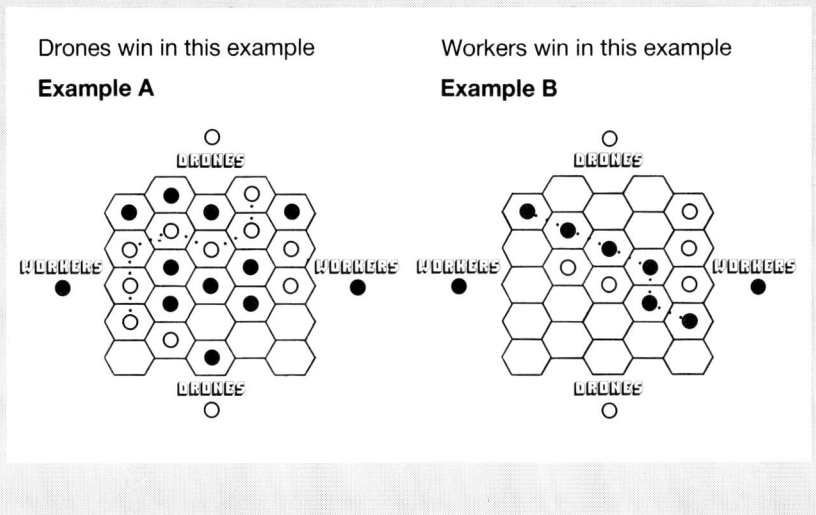

- Play the game a few times.
- Each time you play, write down, on the back of your 'Comments' sheet, whether the 'Workers' or 'Drones' win.

STAGE 1

Looking at other games

Ask your teacher for a copy of this sheet, and fill it in yourself. It will help you to think of other board games you have played.

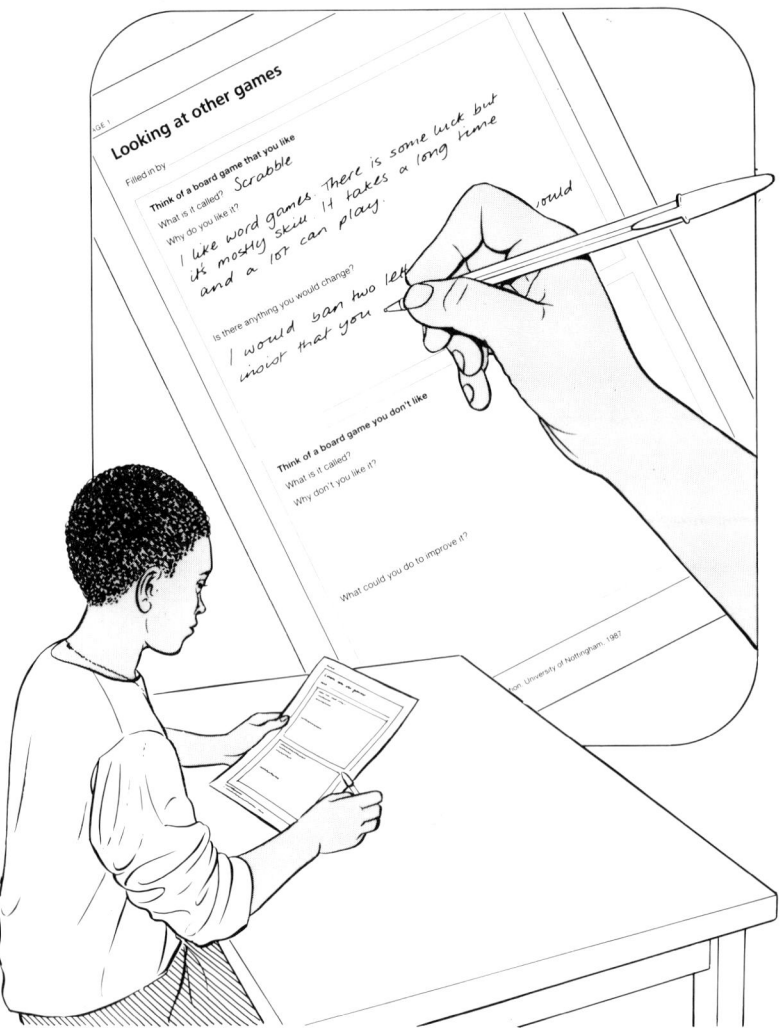

Stage 2 Developing your own ideas

It's easy to spot mistakes in other people's games, but it's quite hard to avoid making them yourself.

In this section your group will invent a new, original game.

This will involve . . .

- Brainstorming,
- Reaching agreement,
- Drawing up a rough plan,
- Testing and improving your plan,
- Getting everything ready.

STAGE 2

Brainstorming

> You will each need a copy of the 'Brainstorming' sheet.
>
> On your own, make lists and draw diagrams to show
>
> - what your game could be about,
> - what the board could look like,
> - what the aim of the game could be,
> - any special features your game could have.

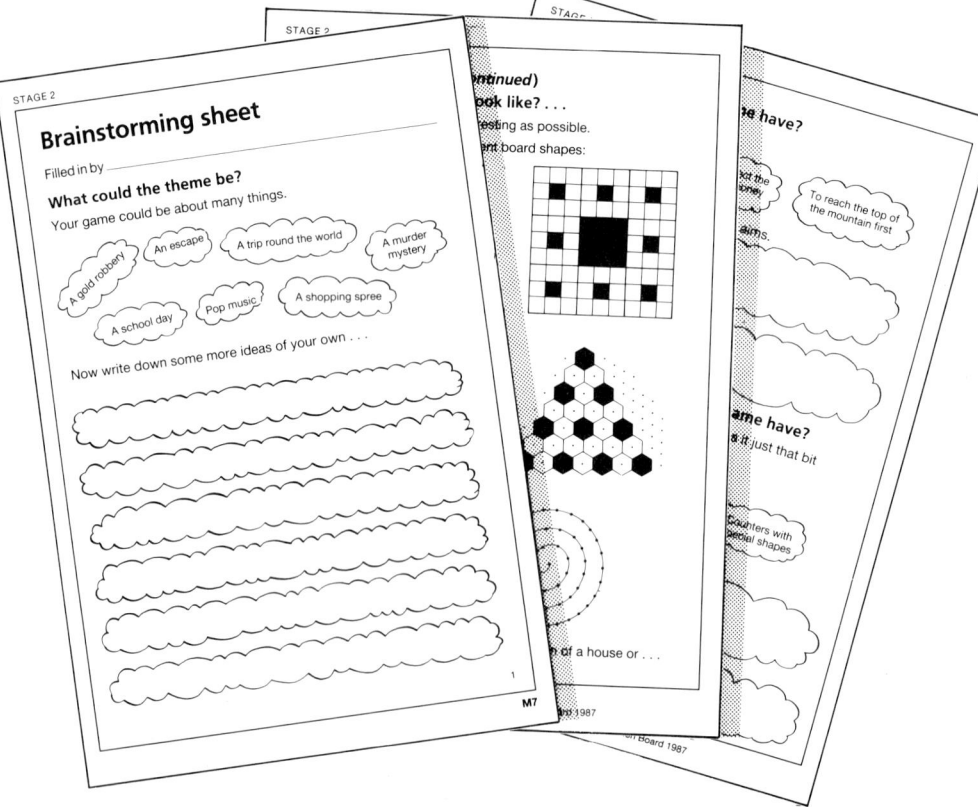

> If you run out of room on your 'Brainstorming' sheet, or if you need any special kinds of paper, then ask your teacher.

STAGE 2

Reaching agreement

Look at all the different lists and drawings your group has produced. Give each person a chance to explain his or her ideas.

Using your lists, try to agree on the details of a game that your group could make. If you cannot agree, then why not produce two games, or two versions of the same game?

Have you agreed on answers to the following questions?

- Who is the game for?
- What will it be about?
- What will the board look like?
- What will be the aim of your game?
- What will you need in order to play it?

If so, then read on . . .

STAGE 2

Drawing up a rough plan

When your group has agreed on your game, each person should fill in the top half of a 'Rough plan' sheet.

Do not worry about writing the rules yet.

Rough plan

Names *Barbara Frazer, Wesley Fisher, David Smith, Catherine Swan*

Our game is called ... *Everest*

Who it's for ...
Four players aged 10 upwards

What you need in order to play ...
Board, 2 dice, 4 counters, spinner

What it's about ...
You have to climb the mountain avoiding accidents.

Aims of the game ...
To be the first to reach the top.

Rules

How to start ...

How to make a move ...

STAGE 2

Now each person should draw a rough design for the board on a separate sheet of paper.

Use pencil, so that you can easily make changes.

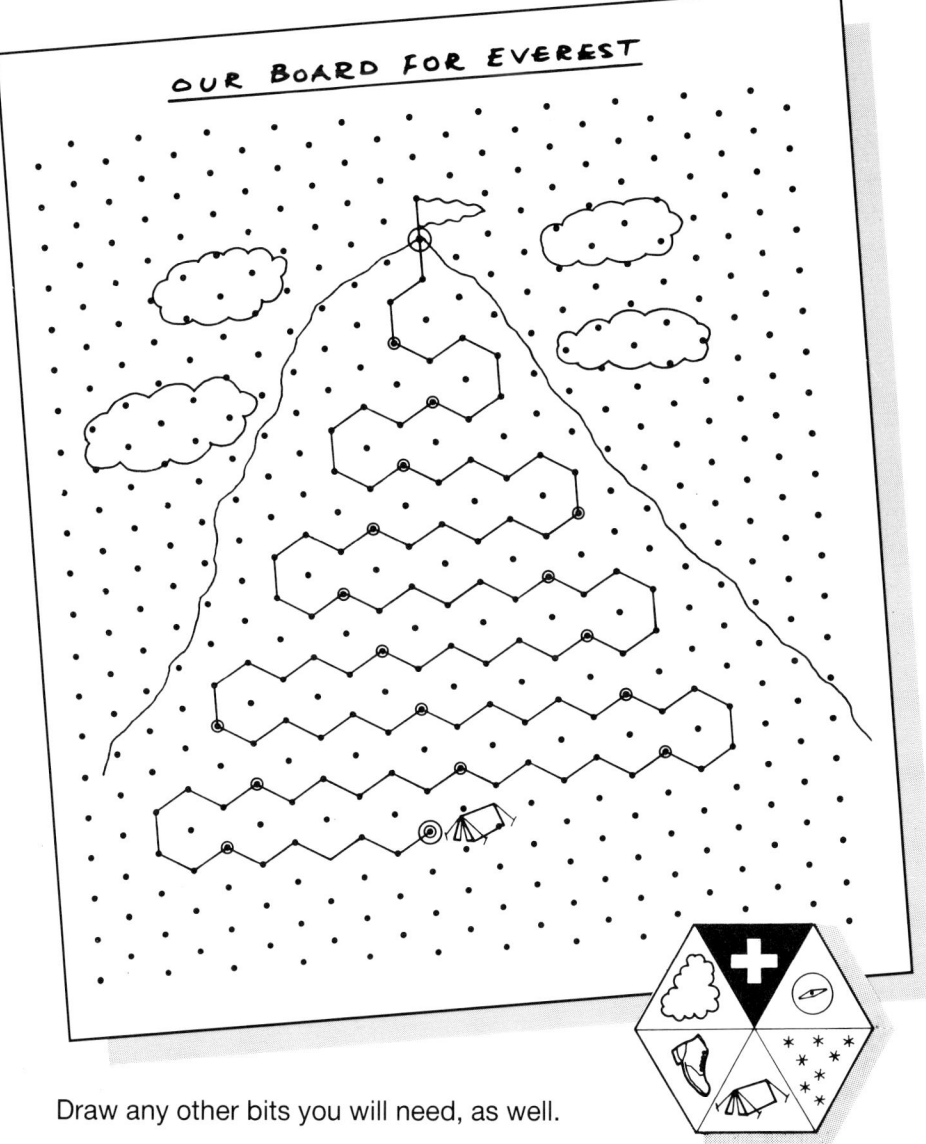

Draw any other bits you will need, as well.

STAGE 2

Write down some rules for your game on a spare piece of paper.

Now try playing the game in your group.

As you play, you will probably think of
- new rules,
- changes to the board,
- ideas for new pieces.

Make a note of all these new ideas.

I can't write rules . . .

Well, you say them out loud and I'll write down what you say.

This game is boring. How can we make it more exciting?

Why don't we give each player *three* counters.

Yes, then each player has to get their team up the mountain first.

I'll write that down.

I know, suppose a team is 'roped' together, so the counters must stay close.

Shall we change the board as well?

Other people have got to be able to play your game by just reading your rules.

Each person should try to write out a good copy of them on the bottom of their 'Rough plan' sheet.

STAGE 2

Testing and improving your plan

When you think your game might work,

either   try it out in your group, *using your rules* to tell you how to play it.

or   give your game to another group and watch them play it.

Think carefully as the game is played. Is there anything wrong with

- the rules
- the board
- the other pieces

?

YES Then change it and try again.

NO Then turn over.

STAGE 2

Getting everything ready

Before you begin to make your game, you will need to collect things like
   scissors, glue, counters, card, special paper, an envelope to put bits in . . .

Make a list of the things you will need.

Make sure that everyone knows what they must bring, especially your teacher!

The following page may help.

What we need	Where from	Who will get it
	home	John
Felt pens		
Counters		Teacher
Scissors	stock cupboard	
Glue		
Cardboard		
Isometric paper		Kathy
	home	everyone
Playing cards	home	
used matches		Rajiv
Ruler	home	
Compass		Barbara (on her way home)
	shops	
Dice		

STAGE 2

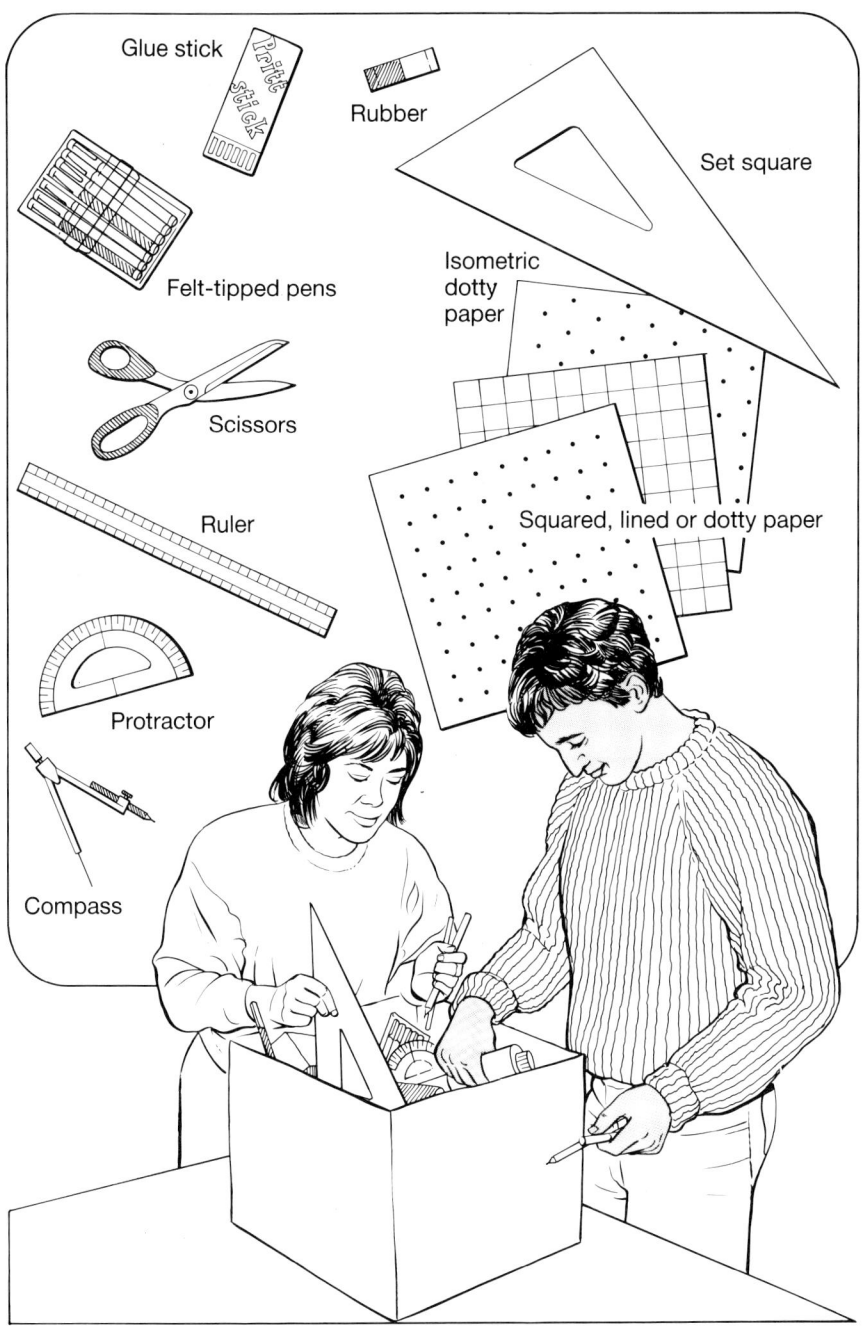

Stage 3 Making your game

In this stage, your group will be involved in

- Making the board,
- Collecting and making any extra bits,
- Writing the final version of the rules.

STAGE 3

Making the board

You now have to make a large, neat, final version of your board.

Before you start, discuss these three questions:

What shape will your board be?

How big will your board need to be?

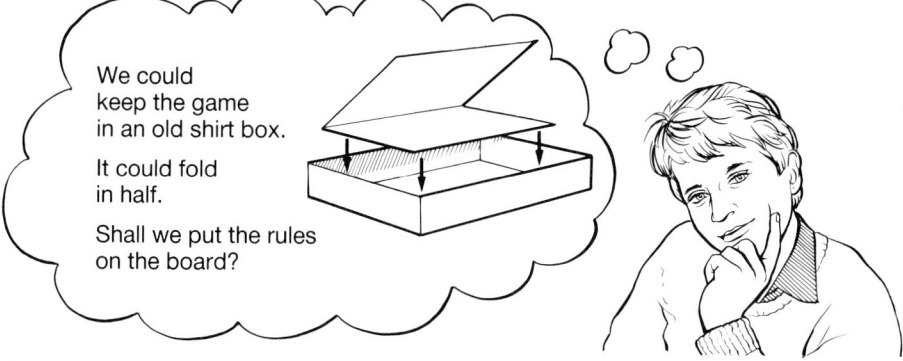

We could keep the game in an old shirt box.

It could fold in half.

Shall we put the rules on the board?

How will you make your board?

Let's draw the board in felt-tipped pen.

But suppose we mess it up?

Could we draw parts of the board onto bits of coloured paper and paste them on?

There are some more ideas over the page . . .

STAGE 3

Here are some ideas which may help you make your board.

If your board contains a lot of shapes all the same, try making a template from tracing paper . . .

1. Draw the shape accurately on tracing paper.

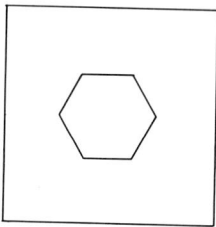

2. Place the tracing paper on the cardboard base.

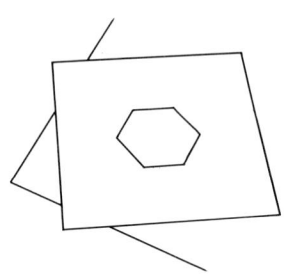

3. Prick through with a pin.

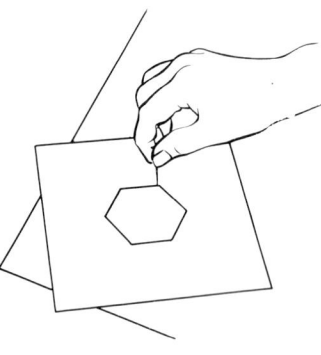

4. Lift off the tracing paper and draw between pin pricks.

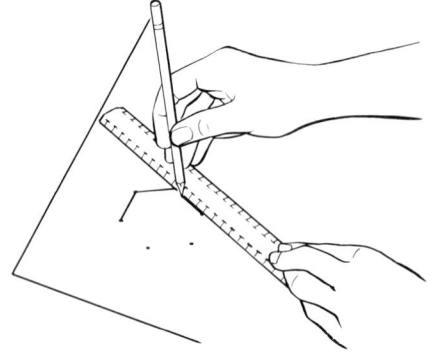

5. Re-position the tracing paper on the base and repeat . . .

. . . until the design is complete.

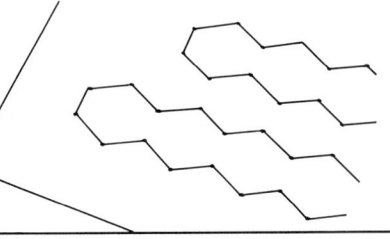

STAGE 3

You could also try making a mosaic board.

1. Draw parts of your board on pieces of coloured paper, using a template.

2. Cut these pieces out and paste them into place.

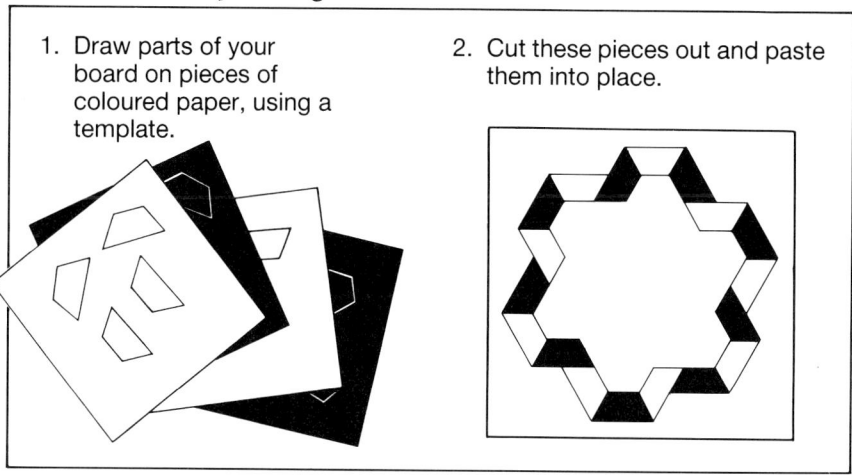

If your board has some kind of symmetry . . .

1. Draw part of your board and trace it.

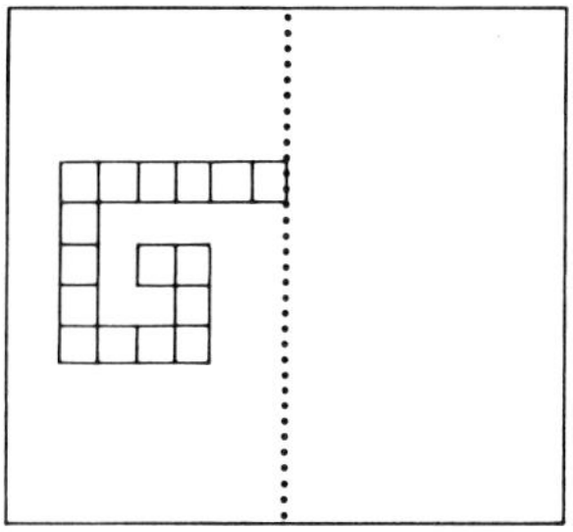

2. Turn your tracing paper *over*.

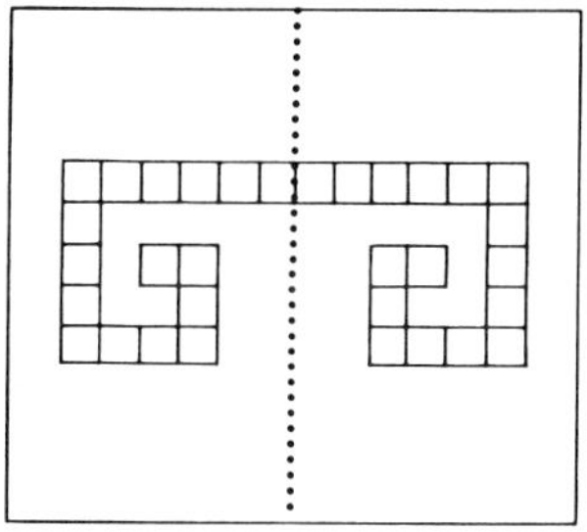

OR

2. Turn your tracing paper *round*.

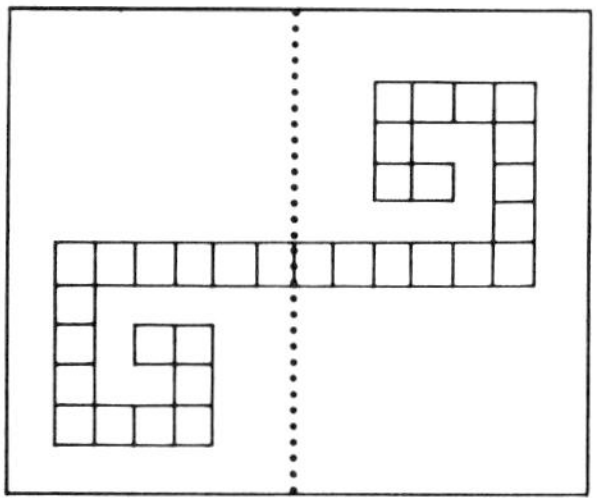

3. Prick through the tracing paper with a pin, and finish the board.

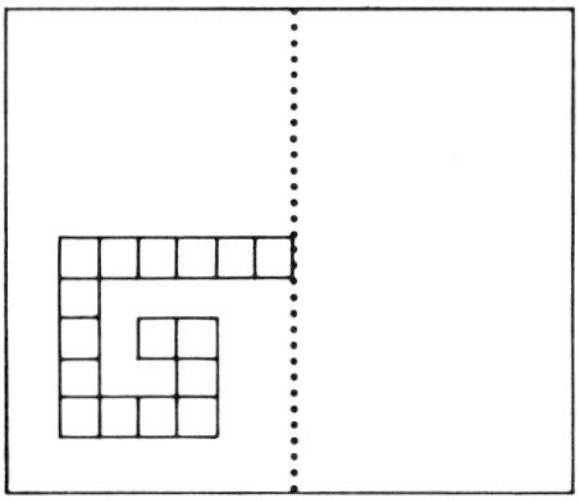

27

STAGE 3

Collecting and making any extra bits

Do you need
- spinners?
- counters?
- dice?
- special cards?
- other bits and pieces?
- something to put bits in?

You may need to buy things like dice, but why not make your own counters or spinners or . . .

Writing the final version of the rules

Play the game just once more, to give your rules a final check. Make sure they are *clear* and *complete*.

What happens now?

It's simple, all you have to do is . . .

Well, why don't the rules say so?

Now write out a neat version of your rules.

You may be able to use a typewriter or word processor.

All finished!   Now it is time to go public!

Stage 4 Testing and evaluating

When several games are finished, swap your game with one from another group.

You will then

- test *their* game to see how well it works,
- see what the other group thinks of *your* game.

STAGE 4

Testing another group's game

Be a fair tester!

- Take time to read and understand the rules, but ... *do not ask* the other group to explain them!
- Play their game.
- As you play, fill in a 'Comments' sheet.
- Say what was good about their game and what they could improve.

STAGE 4

Evaluating your own game

When other groups have played your game,

- read through their 'Comments' sheets.
- compare their comments against your game.
- make any changes you can which will improve your game (including rule changes).

Then, each person should fill in the 'Evaluating your own game' sheet.